WINGS OF A STRANGER

ACKNOWLEDGMENTS

Acknowledgement is made to the editors of the magazines in which the following poems appeared:

Atlanta Review for 'Baptism' and 'Lulu and Seaman';

Blue Milk for 'Stranger', 'A Simple Morning' and 'Predecessors';

DrumVoices Revue for 'Patricia's Lament' (as 'Southern Love') and 'The Myth Keepers';

Wasafiri (London) for 'Chenille', 'Islander' and 'Death of an Uncle'.

ANTHONY KELLMAN

WINGS OF A STRANGER

PEEPAL TREE

First published in Great Britain in 2000
Peepal Tree Press Ltd
17 King's Avenue
Leeds LS6 1QS

ISBN 1 900715 44 9

CONTENTS

PART ONE

Come on, come on, my love.
You're all I'm dreaming of.
Get your bags, get your things, and let's all put on wings,
and we'll dance in the sky up above.

BARBADOS SUNRISE

The island's body flutters to life
with chirping sparrows, warbling doves, squawking crows.
A dog howls in the distance.
A minibus bores down Spring Garden like a moray eel.
The quickening burst quickly ends
and the partially-silhouetted peace of Brandon's beach ripples
at a slow even pace, fanned by gentle casuarinas, our elegant pines.
On the sea's thigh, a cargo barge lay motionless,
sparkling night lights still signaling her rest.

From beneath the balcony of the guest house,
the clack of heels on asphalt. Light increases on a tall brown woman
in burgundy pants-suit forging toward the main road.
Then the other pace, the other tempo: a blackbird slowly pecks
a discarded fast-food carton in the centre of the road.
A sparrow picks at another object on the fringe of the road.
More gently swaying casuarinas above the houses. The heads
of two coconut trees lightly touch each other like a happy couple.

More footsteps. Not the urgent clack of working feet this time,
but a light slapping, a more casual sound:
a couple still wet with the sea. She holds one end of a towel
draped over the shoulder. How admirable, how privileged
to welcome the sunrise from the sea!
Two crows, several sparrows and a redbreast move
silently but purposefully toward the carton
and now there's something, some white sacrament,
in each beak. They hop to the pavement to feed.
Cirrus clouds drift westward. The sky is a web of utility wires.
Light grows sharper by the second. Light
races over pea trees, over twirling orange crotons.
A soaring blackbird fans the air.

A woman in a nurse's uniform strides toward the main road.
Her heels run as the bus comes into view.
The driver toots the horn to tell her he'll wait.
She'll board with a winded thank you. She'll
smile with relief and take her seat.
The plaintive cry of pigeons, ominous and hopeful,
the last thing heard before all darkness disappears
and sunlight once more is fully throned.

LULU AND SEAMAN

Somnambulistic, reclining on a shore's sandy couch,
I inhale the sea's raw wholeness and its ancestral hum.
Slowly, my eyes open, careful not to disturb nature's hold.
Through eyelids winking with light, I read the black letters on
        her nodding prow,
"Lulu." The *Yamaha* outboard's already hoisted up,
the seaman already wading in the water.
He throws the grappling anchor into the shallows
and returns to her. Yanking out a small net fat with fishes,
he hooks and wraps the net's draw-string
around one oarlock. Undulating water softly rinses
the netted buoyant cargo. Seaman reaches into the boat,
withdraws a short spade. Untying the drawstring that slips
from the boat like an eel, he heads for the shore with his load.

Glancingly, he speaks to me, lays down the net like a comma on sand, digs
a deep hole. The dead fishes leap into the crater. He garments them
        with sand,
withdraws a scaling knife with an arc of his hand.
That sandy sheet shields the sun's hardening rays, lightens his task.
One by one, cavali, garfish, snapper and eel are touched by his blade.
Hills of scales, guts and fins rise around his calm, thorough endeavor.
Labor done, he shovels the refuse into the grave, fills it in with sand.
In the background, almonds, sea grapes, and casuarinas line
the beach and punctuate a cloudless
blue sky. Under one waving casuarina, a man holds a bike.
Three boisterous young men cut across the scene.
A white pitbull trots before them, leashless, blind
to its own terror. The man drops his bike and scurries up the tree.
The dog doesn't notice him. The loud ones laugh.
Taking no chances, I rise and leap, headlong, into the sea.

Surfacing in a spurting fountain, I shake water from my eyes,
turn toward shore. The man and his bike are gone.
The young men and the dog, gone.
But Seaman's still there examining his finished work.
He calmly places the cleaned fishes into the net.
Workshop tidied, his ready-to-cook catch wrapped
around an arm, he saunters toward the dry sand and sheltering trees.

In the shallows, grey hulled "Lulu" nods in eternal agreement,
resting her wood, guarding the beach,
the eight-inch steel propeller an asterisk on the sea's blue page.

KING OF TUK

(For Wayne "Poonka" Willock)

Take a penny-whistle for a fife,
a rum barrel for a hand-held bass drum,
a plywood snare hanging off the shoulder
like a pendant of ancestral praise.

Regimented western sounds
are loosened by native skins
bruised but pulsing still
in limestone caverns, under canopies of trees.

Triumphant, this new birth,
triumphant, the songster
who rescued it for the world.
It nods at the blues, waves at the ballad.

Through neighbourhoods teeming
with the young and old,
at fairs, festivals, funerals,
the Creole beat is distinctive

as the summons of a conch.
It calls us to its universal house,
to calypso, classics,
waltzes, yuletide hymns.

Always, we end with the beginning;
end with the sense of primordial
wonder; end with the hope
of regained innocence, like a boat

saying farewell to the sea
that first baptized its hull.
And the end is only sweet
when we see where we've started,

see again every shouldering for selfhood,
every wound gaping for truth
in ourselves, in our ancestors,
in our children whose eyes clutch the future.

To take all this knowledge,
this penny-whistle, goat-skin,
clammy-cherry sticks, salt-meat can
knowledge and steel ourselves, rain or shine,

is to put on the garment of praise,
as a sea rinsing the sides of a boat,
as a flock of cranes flowering a field,
and retell our special story.

Tuk Band rhythm, is all I bring.
Tuk Band rhythm, to make you swing (and swing and swing)

DEATH OF AN UNCLE

You know, Uncle Allan dead for trut'.
No-one had seen or heard from him
for a good few weeks. Every sigh was for
some sign, some scrape of his boot.

Whole weeks he'd slip 'way with his flock:
friends he'd known from the time he was ten.
My thoughts lengthened, then they leavened when
the Welfare named him Mortimer Rock.

I asked, "Who? Don't know no Mortimer."
The Welfare woman gave such richfull
details, they formed into our uncle.
Inside the Home's gray walls, I stood firm

when they removed the cloth to show me
his face. My heart warmed in my chest.
At seventy-nine, he'd lived with just
the right amount of simplicity:

good friends, no wife, now and then, a rum.
My mother said, as a boy, he was proud;
left school early like every poor man child.
He joined a Tuk band and played bum-drum.

His face was firm as a crow's. Our stock,
our history, long, hard and chiseled:
resilient limestone that's peopled
with palms, our uncle Mortimer Rock.

A FATHER'S LAND
(For Amos Favorite, Sr.)

Spanish moss, bayous teeming with crocs,
unbending live-oaks, fenced lots, cattle-grazing pastures;
the pace of shoppers and motorists easy as an islander's,
highway curbs dotted with an occasional dead dog,
possum, deer, to be devoured by sun, by scavenging crows.

On one lot, a two-bathroom, four-bedroom house.
A man, surrounded by four generations, leans
a proud head against an oak rocker.
In the 50s, a planter, determined to die free from his ancestral curse,
offered blacks one-acre lots at seventy dollars an acre.
The wise man bought twelve and a half, planted cotton one year
and paid off what he owed, moved his family from the little house
by the river, slaughtered two hogs a year (the children cleaned the guts,
drained the blood in enamel pans) one for the family,
the other parceled out as gifts to neighbours.

In Ascension, the oldest daughter chose
to attend the all-white school
with its up-to-date curricula. Four
other students who were to join her
retreated when *jim crow* growled.
On Graduation Day, parents and police flanked
her into the hall. All chairs immediately
around were as empty as hate.
The four officers each took a seat
and looked about to see if trouble had come.

Later that evening, angry hordes arrived at his home.
"They came to get me, you know. I let off a few rounds,
and they scampered like rabbits. They left their dynamite right there
on that lawn and ran. They were planning to bomb us out, you know.
But I stood up to them. That's how you get respect."

Today, one son occupies an adjacent lot.
The other ten acres recede into woods
where rabbits, coons, and deer try to outfox poachers.
Gunfire cracks the canopies; dogs release collective yelps.
In the yard overgrown with grasses and shrubs,
vines strap a rusted tractor to the earth.

Human strength lessens even as children pulse,
barefooted, in the yard, in the house, on top great grandpa's knees.
Thanksgiving emerges from longevity wrapped
in the voices of many generations. The wise man's
hearty laughter knits past and future together.

ROOFS OF YORKSHIRE

What are those birds circling the roofs of Yorkshire?
Seagulls in for winter, frowning crows, two-hued magpies.
What are they thinking? What are they saying?
We reflect your beings, body and soul.
We mirror racial hatreds, racial hopes,
over Yorkshire, over deciduous birches plainly poised,
over rowans budding for spring,
over dry-stone walls.

For centuries, birds and walls course
through the hills of north of Leeds,
around unhurried villages where garlands
of millstones, spotted with moss,
whose grits once crushed corn to flour a village,
are precise as pyramids and as resolute.

One seeks to compose a verse so tightly packed,
so naturally united, out of one's own plainness:
long stretches of sandy beach,
rows of cane rustling with crows and cranes,
long runways of singing surf.

ISLAND

Island is a womb in a cave;
island is a wave inside me.
By the seashore, I will come back again,
and the pain of the strain of the rain in my heart
will be no more.

Island is the light in my name.
Island is your body rising from the sea,
rinsing my mind with the juice of your hair,
dancing on the water, blue water everywhere.

Island is a caged sun.
Island is a brown girl, is a brown girl
sturdy and strong. Island is a blue song:
sad coruscating chords of victories won.

Island is the water in my name
coasting round St. Lucy,
down through them St. John hills,
coursing through to St. Peter,
ruk-a-tukking to St. Michael.

Island is the light in my name.

PART TWO

My drowning arms flay all around that should be loving you instead,
You drew me out, you warmed me, took me over the water's edge.

STRANGER

Even when I lived here, my gaze on this rock
intense as a crow's, I often felt outside of things.
Not the warbling surf or the flamboyant's
lolling tongues sounding castanets in the teeth of the wind;
not the slow grazing cattle that taught me patience,
taught me how not to waste energy blindly lashing at flies
but to wait for that one rare moment to dance with death;
not the linguistic loveliness of sparrows and wood doves,
flirtatious, self-conscious, every chirp a lyric,
but the absence of human touch.

Long ago, I had such closeness,
before the shame of poverty and fear of its exposure;
before the hauling pains of poetry,
before Crop Over masks and the shallows of sorrow:
the matriarch's sudden parting, the patriarch's untimely death,
the siblings' flight from sun to snow and another death.

I reasoned this to be art's exile.
Still, I desired to be touched by hands, not just those rising with sea salt
or glowing with the hibiscus' thick red palette.
I had my store of metaphors which I would gladly have traded
for a dialogue in flesh and blood,
the concrete thing and not merely its symbol,
however filled with oceanic grace.

I craved contact beyond the surface of how-you-do,
beyond the professional acquaintances and acceptances,
the lively lonely reception rooms, the blank faces,
the cuteness of friends and lovers,
the political correctness in a world where, like that of the spy,
nothing's as it seems, and you never know the truth
of what's truly felt or really believed.

So before khus-khus pierced the heart,
we piled into a rented van for our Saturday angelus
in the country where the patriarch was born.
Aunts and uncles, all smiles, hugged us, said how big we'd grown.
After home-cooked eating, the grown-ups spoke
of those who'd passed on: Uncle Ossie, Aunt Dottie.
Remembered their smiles or brows scowling with grief.
We sat silent, absorbing the past into our flesh, our bones.

Throbbing with the ages, we'd go into the yard, run 'bout,
indulge in ripened grapefruits and oranges dangling
like ornaments on a Christmas tree. And if we couldn't reach them,
someone offered his back for a ladder.
And if some fruit evaded us still, we'd climb the tree...

On Sunday after church, the patriarch headed
the table where we gathered like almonds round a coast
rustling with thanks and shared love passed around in bowls
of rice and peas, beef stew, baked chicken and roasted pork,
steamed beans, avocado and cucumber salad,
the steam from the table coiling upwards like prayers.

Once, on the porch after dinner, I saw a group
of brown butterflies journeying over the garden
like a pattern of sky-divers challenging gravity.
Their wings seemed to touch each other, to support each other.
And I knew the truth in what I saw.

In an alien hour, yearning for such tactile moments,
I remember those wings,
see myself borne on their fluttering, buoyant tips.
And the sight of that glory is enough
to sustain me in my flight.

PICTURES FROM A ROCK

1

From mid-morning to dark, the sea soothed our adolescent days.
Tourists were non-threatening, oddities on the landscape.
Very present. Very distant. Objects visually ingested and quickly forgotten.
No one pondered over their origins or the nature
of their lives. We had our own ways and obsessions,
our own humor. Like the jokes about the Queen.
Did she wipe her own bottom? Did she stool gold?
Half-believing, we rolled with laughter
like effervescing waves, hooked forefingers
to the corners of our mouths, pulled fully outward, and tried to say:
"The Queen's brass bowl," while palms rustled
around the wooden houses.

2

In high school, it's hard to hold such simplicities,
hard to keep friends who once protected me, now dropped out,
diminished through drugs, violence, abuse.
The widening gulf signals the end of an age
to which a part of me still clings.
What to do? Which way to turn?
A branch snaps from the croton tree.
The coiled dry leaves fall.

3

I'm nineteen. I'm one hundred.
Child of Imagination. Child of society.
Broken, withdrawn, gray.
No middle-class friends, no lower-class friends.
Just the staring into the wide mouth of the sea,
the same sea that held my youth like cargo,
that holds me now in a year of darkness.

Middle-aged child of Imagination, child of society,
what's the nature of pain on an island rock?
That which is unnatural like a palm tree with a maple's accent,
like a mahogany aping an oak or chestnut.
Wandering north, what is the strength away from strength?
Memories of cresting seas, a landscape dotted with palms,
limestone dwellings, trellised chattels,
casuarinas doing their rustling dance.

ANOTHER ISLAND

The sides of the interstate are swollen with pines.
The infinite greens pulse like those famed parted walls
of water, waiting for the word to fall.
Deciduous maple and sweet gum sparkle
between green layers in rust brown, ochre,
flaming red, distressful orange, sharp malarial yellow.
Kudzu has finally loosened its hold;
its collapsed body blends with mounds of dried leaves
while deep beneath the soil roots cling to the future.

Sandwiched by such natural laws,
I cross the causeway to St. Simon's Island.
I know a place, where I come from,
whose tone is as pleasurably remote,
where the bark of city life peels easily away,
and simplicities – two lovers strolling on the waterfront,
black women hooking fish from a jetty,
surf breaking over rocks – slow the pulse rate,
allows me to hold time in my right hand.

In the hotel's courtyard, a running fountain claps
the short side of the still-active pool.
Water ripples strongly there, lightly elsewhere.
An elderly man with a bald dome draped at the base
with grey hair, loose as unwound violin strings, leans over the daily.
Today's headlines, the mayoral results.
Behind him, at a curiously safe distance,
an elderly woman reclines in a lounger with her paperback.
Politics and paperbacks. The safe distance.
The woman, also greying, wears a hint of red dye in her thin hair.
Man and wife? They sit so relaxed,
so comfortably timeless, so comfortably separate.

The gazebo's flanked on one side by sterile banana trees.
On the other, by two large oaks, Spanish moss dripping
like the unkempt moustaches of Civil War soldiers.
Two pines erupt from the azalea hedge
so close I can reach out and touch them. No bloom in the hedge.
Only one shining thing lay at an angle on the ocean of leaves.
A *Coors* can, flung, no doubt, by someone from above.
It nestles there, like old age, like exile,
used and discarded yet still determined to shine.

THE TREE'S ARM

The climber anchors himself to a main branch,
pulls the chain saw to life,
prunes fingertips of leafless branches
that touched the sky for seventy years,
reaches for lower limbs still choked with ivy.
Enraged, cheated, by death, of total possession,
the ivy laps and staples the trunk.
Two days later, branches, like so many made irrelevant,
are claimed by gravity. Dead armies of brush line
the sidewalk, waiting for the roaring furnace.

Five fingers sprout from what's now a hand,
the whole arm raised, not in defiance, but surrender.
The ground crew advances in strides.
One loops a rope round a finger.
One will saw each finger into transportable lengths.
Another will lug them to the truck.
The tree-strapped climber tears off ivy
the way a man removes feathers
from a chicken's neck before slicing it with a knife.
The roper on the ground says, 'I'm all set.'

From his perch, the climber tests the line one last time,
then bursts into labour, slicing the finger with loving precision.
Decelerated by the rope's tension,
it swings backwards and forwards.
Two men ease it to the ground as the roper gives let.

Three fingers are severed this way.
The crew loop rope around thumb and remaining fingers,
tighten the pulley attached to a dogwood.
Now on the ground, the climber carves the base.
With each cut, crewmen draw the pulley tighter,
hang like human clothes pegs from the far end of the line,
pushing backwards and downwards
for increased pressure and weight.

The arm finally cracks like a large tree struck by lightning.
As a fallen president, it thunders to the lawn,
gouging a deep crater, trying to bury itself.
The climber throws himself next to his trophy, exhausted and proud.
The roper backs the truck to the edge of the lawn
to receive the final logs.

Then sudden rain and smiles of relief.
The ritual's ended. Another conquest.
Tomorrow, another place.
I'm left here with the sadness and lost.

DOWNTOWN LEEDS

We leave working-class King's Avenue,
with its back-to-back terraced housing created
for blue collars decades ago, and cruise
into the city with its acceptance of free trade.
Yet, Balti, MacDonald's and Toys R Us
do not extinguish Yorkshire ale,
Yorkshire pudding, or Yorkshire cricket.
These ikons cement a place to its past
as Banks beer, cou-cou, and cricket
do in Barbados. Our task, wherever we are,
is to find some symbol parallel to what we know.
It could be as tangible as Macs, or a mood, a color.
It places us everywhere at once, as Janus, as Tawarawa.

Downtown, crowds are coated, gloved.
They file past Yorkshire Bank, pass Lloyds
to or from lunch-breaks. I search
each face for any distinguishing marks.
Does a people reflect a landscape?
Is landscape mirrored in a people?
This city seems fixed in neutrality, packed together
like dry stone walls without the intimacy.
Temperatures low and glazed with sunlight,
this isn't Georgia with its inability to be sure
(winter-in-spring; spring-in-winter; summer in spring).
The faces here betray nothing, are calmly locked,
softly blank and neutral. Uninviting yet not unfriendly.
Ageless certainty. Contentedly private.
Intimate or not, I'm drawn by such stability, such honesty.
So I join the geography of souls hedging the sidewalk,
our arms only uniting like the difficult branches of privet.

THE MYTH KEEPERS

High in the mountains near Cullowhee,
spreading five acres at the base
of Mingo Falls, eleven thousand Cherokees gather.
They hold history in lined tightly-drawn faces,
how the land was lost, how they regain these few acres,
how they make their own decisions again
through the tribal chief and his council.

Mary Little John has always lived under these canopies
of pine and spruce, through which rivers run
and rapids sound ancestral names.
At the reservation's entrance, welcoming signs
declare "authentic Cherokee craft."
"Our main economy here is tourism," says Mary.
"Soon, the gambling casinos will open.
Most are for it. Our chief is pushing for it."

Her cousin points to the Cherokee Dependency Center,
her people's Betty Ford. They stagger from camps
all across the country to these healing hills
to the eternal soothe of water whose sound hums
within the frond-covered bosom of the mountains.

Half a mile inside where tourism no longer follows,
Mary pulls the red Rover onto a gravel embankment.
She points to a water hole and the foaming shallow rapids
where they played as children.
I am stirred by the clarity of water.

A trout farm, swimming into view,
completes the town. We head back to the tourist center.
Sequoyah's bust erupts in regal cedar from the museum's front lawn.
Inside, I open up and embrace the origins of fire.
I expose myself to the sound of that flame and hear a familiar ring.
It telegraphs south through Antillean air
to Dominica's fern-wrapped hills,

to Guyana winged with dreams of gold
where the same ancestors who'd sailed the Behring Straits
brought their stone and iron culture,
their adzes and bonehead arrows,
their bone flutes and canoes chiseled
from the shanks of trees.

Outside, in the Teepee Restaurant, I calmly chew
bean balls, collard greens, and fried chicken,
the first, Cherokee; the last two, typically Southern.
And I think of home, of cornmeal and okra cou-cou
with bits of cavali swimming in the centre.
It was the bean balls' cornmeal that roused such remembrances,
such feelings of hybridity and connectedness
to the damned and the blessed.

THE MASTERS

1

The same magnolia leaves perfectly glazed.
The same frothing dogwood, same elegant greens.
A fraternal vice grips the city, subject
to neither God or man.

Laughter, if not properly pitched,
will wilt the ceremonial green,
make the well-pruned dogwoods frown.
Such external lucency! Such careful glittering illusions!

From those locker rooms, humming beneath
like living catacombs, to the black
man gathering refuse above,
it's crucial to know how to walk,
how to talk and do Dixie.

After Charles Sifford and Pete Brown knocked in vain,
Lee Elder teed-off, elegantly non-white.
Now, two black members grace the sacred verdure
sentried by neo-plantation buildings
that stare nostalgically into the past,
while, not far away, slithers Washington Road,
tawdry and pimpled with fast foods.

2

School's out and the delicate blue sky
rings with profit. The NAACP, weary with waiting, notes:
"For over sixty years, those oaks have dropped
sanctimonious leaves to fertilize their own grass."
Mere preservation of tradition?
But why does one feel a chill in this Southern heat
when those stiff green jackets pass?

To own a green jack,
to feel its gentle writhing round the shoulders.
One aspirant sighs with grief
as the white ball slips into its watery grave.
No green cloth will wrap those shoulders this year.
Up the fairway, others inhale hopeful air
and thank their god for privilege.
A black caddie, all smiles, dressed in white,
chips behind.

3

Then comes Woods the tiger.
A white caddie, godhead grim and gray,
chips behind him. By the second day,
faces are starched with tension
and, soon, with unbelief. The tiger wears the green jacket.
While History cannot forget itself,
rulers and their followers will.
Already, the true sound of that roar is denied
its symbolic height and depth that should
occasion an embrace of all tigers, not just one.
In the end, it's just another year, another act
in this city's extravagant play
for the privileged masters of the city.

BETWEEN TWO CITIES

I wake expecting to see a purple ceiling and four petalled lights,
to hear a cardinal's soft swooping sigh
and the low hum of Atlanta.
Instead, a scraping light coughed up
by a golf-scarred city scratches me.
Most of me is elsewhere,
and that brief deception's all I need
to know where I don't belong.
From that shaken moment, I saw home
as the certainty of light
(however muted; however loud)
but never rough like sandpaper.

PATRICIA'S LAMENT

A man containing all my blood's admonished virtues.
A man naive (as till now, I was) to my depth of racial unease.
Lunches. Dinners. I wore a normal face.
At his birthday party, I swelled with admiration and stuck to him.
After every guest had gone, we kissed, fondled, and were ready.

But that ancient southern spirit yanked me round,
spoke, at length, into my ears,
and I couldn't... I couldn't.

So I kneaded him till he came, then snuggled
unhappily, knowing I could've had it all
but for my cursed consciousness.

Sleep hauled us in.
His snoring woke me, and I left.
When dawn's stabbing light thrust
through my curtained window, I shuddered once,
sensed him look around,
sensed him frown at my empty space.

PORTRAIT

The Southern moon's in her blood.
She seeks a golden gate,
marries her college prince, breathes
for him, and knows, too late,

that love for self is wise.
Thirty now, she holds the school
gate with calloused hands,
pondering life as cruel.

Determined to restore
those lost years, she'll bring
to class her young children
and let her presence ring.

She sighs for the girl near her.
Nothing here has changed. The aim's
still to gain a tiara
and arrive at wisdom through pain.

CHENILLE

She did what they required.
The last glad word,
'scholar,' moves them, but still she wants.

Always breathing islands,
struggles to a coast,
cultures clashing yet congruous.

Plunged in exile, frowning,
manners are her dance.
Faces fix to access her chant:

an honest tone, a line
that's fresh as pine,
normal, holy, a fist of earth.

Chenille will always string
her hair. She'll drink
from a liberal sharing cup.

ISLANDER

Fluttering, rummaging islander,
Listen, I tell you, hold on to the shore.
With your mind, seize the new stone
over where a seaswell leavens like a womb.

When the coursing sun is a carrion bird
winded with hate, heading seaward,
All those seagrapes, verdant shields,
will fence your experimental fields.

Woman, cross-legged like a coiled
dancer on her guard wall,
throws back, just once, her croton hair,
then falls through some he-light's melting stare.

She will need to seize new stone.
She will limp while walking in blood.
Pain both ways and which is worse?
It's the way of sunlight, its scowling cost.

PRESSURE

A man, slapping, slicing imagi-
nary partners, lands on glistening
exceptional sand, starts smiling in
the salt-heavy glazed austerity

around this shore. Greying, another
man beats sand like builders' hammering.
I hear thuds where hands and water ring.
I see throbbing muscles (from my recliner).

A slim woman peddles the air.
She stares skyward, peddling on her back.
Assurance is right here on this track
of sand. Hand going down deep, I conjure

from soft balled sand, globes that're breathing still.
My hand twitches with every black
necessity. Each globe is attacked,
destroyed, to be rebuilt at my will.

PREDECESSORS

One April, in St. Philip where Nanny Grigg' s voice mingled
with the blackbird's volatile squawk,
I witness an ancient mahogany laid to rest.
The stump of its once regal trunk is all that remains,
a plant pot eight inches deep, wide with imperial rot.
I fill it with ferns; watch them waterfall down its sides.

Now, I gaze over salt-laden days,
over limestone acres where Nanny no longer speaks.
I see the severed heads of palms
from whose hurricane-razed trunks dry moss extends:
un-regenerative blight ringing our shores.

One April, in St. Phillip where Nanny Grigg's voice mingled
with the blackbird's volatile squawk,
I witness an ancient mahogany laid to rest.
The stump of its once regal trunk is all that remains.

PART THREE

Firefly, with a backpack on your shoulders,
you're filled with stars, you're an endless day.

PASTORAL

Bursting through forests of clouds ominous as El Greco's,
the plane turns and beaks again. A horizon, hooded
    with magenta and gold,
announces England's sunrise. Morning lights sparkle like gold dust
I'd once seen flecking the face of a prominent Ivory Coast woman
on the cover of *National Geographic*.
Memories of London in the mid seventies
was a place of wealth, hustling feet, idealistic
art, Osibisa, Donovan, Labi Siffre's
creole strum. At Drury Lane's Theatre Royal, Cat Stevens.
It was a time of flowers sprouting from the breast
of every wino sipping a brown bag and looking to the east.

So the English had their pot of gold.
The only gold I saw on the tube to King's Cross
shone from the mouth of a black woman who spoke
and jested with her East Indian friend. The rest were lost
in one stolid scowl which no imagination could reverse.
At the train station, I paid 50 p to pee. The 56 quid
from London to Leeds wasn't the worst
of it. Nothing was complimentary; not even a coke.

Strange, as the train headed north from Central London,
how light increased and blueness broke from above.
The neat occasional cottage nestled like a hope
in a flat open field ringed with horse chestnuts,
could be Louisiana in spring. Only there, a crow
would perch on pecan branches hefty with leaves,
the temperature 77 degrees, not 37.

It was the pace of things, the slow verdant
motion, like almond trees pulsing in a line,
that made me think such bucolic sap
may yet restore the modern mind.

WINTER WONDER

All cares are capped with snow
and laughter of a tropical child realizing a dream
of snow-covered lawns and snowball fights with Dad.
The balls crack open like island laughter, wide and echoing.
Two inches fell just days before she would leave to dream again.
For now, she's contented to hold this moment:
"Let's build a snow baby, Daddy!"
So we journey over the front lawn with eager hands,
our footprints following us like remembrances....
A conical body. A little round head.
Two black dogwood berries for eyes, twigs for arms.
A red ribbon rescued from Christmas wrappings, a glittering scarf!

WINTER LIGHT

The oaks have shed their leaves.
The skeletons twist and curve like the thoughts of all exiles.
Behind them, downtown buildings raise aphoristic
upper bodies in white, gray, and pink: the Peachtree Tower,
Marriot, Georgia Pacific.
And it's hard to tell who holds ultimate power.
The triumvirate reaches? Or the washy blue sky that drapes them?

Between naked oaks and redbrick steps,
a white wooden house is roofed in gray, chimney nostrilled
        toward heaven.
Utility wires snake from poles through dogwoods and sweet gum.
One dogwood sentries the steps, choiceless
in its deference to the holly's evergreen glory.
Holly fingers it with smiling malevolence,
torturing its side. Dogwood must change.
Stripped bare in one season, it flowers in the next.
Its rootedness its only certainty.

In the porch, Asian chimes tinkle in the breeze
undaunted by wailing ambulance or police.
When those sad sirens fade, chimes tinkle still
like hollies, dogwood roots,
warbling doves and blue jays,
leap of squirrels from tree to scuttling roof...

In the evening news, death saturates the anchor's
voice. Such sad tones from so polished a lyricism:
a six year-old beauty queen raped and strangled,
a six-year old school girl hit-and-run victim,
a missing wife, the abusive husband weeping for the world,
an Ethiopian runner jailed for murdering his cousin
who rejected a union he'd arranged.
No winner in this week's lottery.

Yet, every season has its light.
At night, when I stand on redbrick
steps and look toward the city, light beams
from the three towers of commerce through the ribs
and arms of oaks. In a brighter season, those lights would never be seen.

BLESS YOU, THANK YOU

Spring punches winter with the groundhog's determined nibble.
There's steady sunlight and sixty-five degrees.
In the bank this Friday morning, a man, affable
with his patrician nose, tries to cash four checks
payable to his one-year-old son.
He details the infant's party to a quizzical teller who waves
"Just a minute, please" to drive back this clot in her day.
She must speak with her supervisor. The man fidgets
good-naturedly aware of his unusual request.
His eyes turn and catch mine.
He flushes with self-consciousness, so I nod and smile.
I glimpse a falling-off of some of his stress.
My cashier, hair dripping braids, goes to the check machine.
Soon, I feel an insistent nasal tingling. I reach
for a handkerchief, brace for the stertorous roar.
"Bless you!" someone shouts far across the room.
"Thank you!" I say and recall Grand-dad's atavistic sneeze.
He comforts me now. Better out than in. Never jail
what's natural. How strange, how beautiful
the civility of strangers, their pronouncement of blessing.
We motivate one another in this way. We affirm
our own vulnerability. Empathetic tears
may be a nod, an ancestor prodding
from the grave, an alien voice never heard before.
And that blessing, once given, restores each
blesser as it reassures the blessed.

A FEAST OF WORMS

I watch winter's flesh wrinkle and melt.
Burnished April creeps up the sky's ladder.
The yard's green carpet is laid out for a welcome.
From each bed, I collect last year's pine straws, last year's exclamations,
bag them, and seize the shovel. On the redbrick terrace,
packets of seeds are laid out like resolutions:
zinnia, lavender, foxglove, cucumber, sweet pepper, okra.
Neighbouring them, nestled in little green plastic pots
like newborns in a crib, tomato, eggplant, oregano, sage, mint.
With eager wings, blue jays, cardinals, doves, and redbreasts, gather
on the fence. Their feathered heads dart from side to side.
They exchange positions. All this movement, but one common theme:
something about a feast of worms.

Shovel in hand, I approach the first bed,
thrust in the blade, turn the soil,
shake out the clods with the blade and my hand.
The earth runs with worms.
Some are sliced in half. Those that remain whole,
wriggle with good fortune and fear and perhaps rage.
I have disturbed their feast. And, as I move toward another bed
to happily continue my work, the winged celebrants
fall on earth's plate and pluck the worms away.

My rhythm's constant now; bed after worm-teeming bed:
pierce and turn the soil, shuffle it, loosen it with the shovel,
my hand, let the worms writhe and pour out like blood.
Let the birds rejoice.
Later, I make furrows, bury the seeds and lightly firm.
In ten days, they'll rise.
I look at the hands that bury them,
at the foot that stamps the shovel to make the grave.
One day, I'll find my place
in such rich earth where birds cannot reach,
where seeds root and come to new life,
a feast for worms.

A SIMPLE MORNING

My skin tingles under shaving cream and the blade's even hand.
Here on my jaw is history's grass.
It dies. It grows. Always in motion.
Showered with hope, I clap cologne to my body, dress....
A mug of coffee black as Civil Rights and needed still.
That votive steam contains its own language of freedom,
a softly turning sense of a motion that is peace.
It fills the room with its coiling glory and quickens me.
Outside, a yellow frangipani wraps two lovers with its perfume.
A little girl skips in the driveway.
I refill myself with blackness.
The 9.00 a.m. Caribbean News sounds from a corner.
I draw a chair to the window.
Sunlight dissolves the shadows.
I hum for every simple pleasure.

COMING HOME

1

Exiled thirty-something
years, he rolled with sweat
for a northern national rail.

Smiling "morning" daily,
gained some small respect.
Homegrown ethics will soften stares:

hard work, honest words, soft
answers. Then the test:
his girl's mom and the frowning dad.

Speaking only French, her
parents let him sit.
Pensive, stolid, they heard his lines.

Poitier, he wasn't.
Buoyant in his bright-
ness, he cut an incisive path

for a march of triumph.
Shortly, like the clouds,
hesitancies all evanesced.

2

They worked and saved like ants.
One day his wife
collapsed. Her job turned dark and sour.

Hospitalized, the tests
would yield advanced
diabetes. Within that hour,

all utterances held
epiphany.
Every shadow hummed with dread.

With skins wound tight as strings,
they headed south
bound for Bim, his palm-ringed homeland.

3

Coming in, gliding with the egret's
smooth and glancing grace,
the airplane drops. Hearts beat louder,
shout, "We're home! We love this kind weather!"
Coloured with a new and darker skin,
as a seaman unfurls his skein,
reeled out, reeled in, deep and wide,
eyes fixed like a crow's and bright as a child's.
In this landscape he'd once
known and claimed and held, often getting lost
within each overarching
cavern of comfort, limestone's reckoning,
he's nailed to a past that was always his future.
Away from dread of cold, of fire
(pressing, stressing, damning wild),
their goal's now to plant and build a new life.

4

He's a clammy-cherry branch
amidst the jeers sniffing out their accents.
A beach bum openly solicits her:
"She won't marry you. All she want is a big bamboo."
Celine screams, "We were married in a church, damn you! Didn't your
parents teach you any manners? You don't have any respect?"
Her French tongue rolls with the difficult
English syllables spoken quickly and with rage.
Malcolm reaches for the beach bag: "You better move out my face.
I got a knife in here that can go six inches to your heart."
The intruder, dark skin calloused by too much salt, sun, and sin,
grins and recedes like a crab awkward in his deliberate casualness.
The heaving surf applauds his defeat
then settles its turquoise welcoming mat.

5

Paynes Bay where he berthed
for twenty-seven years
squats east. Lucy is to the west

where his people laugh and
cry and celebrate,
sandwiched, cushioned, by heaven's air.

Nestled, calmly settled,
coral whispering
wind-like, life is a crisp blue sky.

Votive crotons wriggle
skyward, marigolds
gather, certain of happy days.

Planting okra spinach
eggplant with eager hands,
peace comes, rest comes, at last. At last.

RAINBOW OF SAND

A day blaring red heat steadily.
Many-colored choruses
of surf calling. Stand still if this is
your way. Water, surround me.

The saltwater god made several
healthy: man broke arthritic
hinges; tourists part wet lips
in thanks; others drink their belly full.

My mind, cleaned out, watches everyone
playing with love's various
faces, so incongruous,
yet cast in bronze, perfect as the sun,

perfect as the water in the sun
in whose shallows fleeting fish
rumple the sea's linen with their kiss
and leave, for me, a rainbow of sand.

PART FOUR

O yes, I want to reach a mountain,
and I'll reach it from the ground,
so the roots will be real-real strong,
and that's the reason why I'm singing.

BAPTISM

A small congregation gather on faith's lapping shore.
The pastor robed in black.
Two large umbrellas hover above them like halos,
yellow and blue washes repealing the sun's steady strokes.
The hands that hold them cannot be seen, like those
which steadied Peter before he sank with doubt.
Two female candidates, hands clasped before them, wait
like hesitant doves in pink and green gowns,
plastic bath caps, and seaborne faith.
Their eyelashes are flittering hummingbirds' wings.

The choral leader slips away, then turns
with her raised conductor's hand. Caroling melodies rise and mingle
with the surf's wide-ranging tones. Every voice sustains its song.
Every heart intones some blessing.
The pastor moves towards water,
praying hands stretched over the blue conversion zone.
Little darts of light turn in the salt-heavy breezes
and in the lightly cresting waves around me.

He faces shore like Hannibal his mountain,
summons a candidate with the curve of a hand.
One woman nudges the other to send the sea-green turtle
inching across sand to her destiny.
Confidence swelling, she enters water. The pastor reaches
out, steadies her, readies her
for the touch of eternity. One hand on her forehead,
the other on the neck's nape, he guides her, in one well-watered movement,
backwards and under, then hoists her up into a new birth
of spirit and fire.

Emboldened, the second candidate strides toward water,
then falters at the last moment.
Alternately cringing and flailing her arms, she totters
before steadying herself. Finally, she gives

in to the will of the water and of the fire,
is wholly submerged. Emerging from the sea's womb,
she feels the scales of worldliness flake from her,
she hears the watery applause of all heaven's hosts.

On the shore, singing crests, then breaks into clapping hands
and arms raised in rapturous praise.
The pastor wades toward the shallows
as if heading for shore. Suddenly,
he throws himself face-down in the water,
his robe swelling with air pockets. He rises and falls two times more.
He is ready to sail. He is ready to fly.
A parakeet, winged with light, lifts into the salt-heavy air.
The surf and the wind whisper Jesus.

THE HOUR OF FAITH

The jetliner arcs and beaks toward the runway like a heron.
A stanza, white as meringue, blots each window.
I feel Chicago's subzeroes through sight alone.
As I push against air pressure within the exit shaft,
cold fingers try to touch me to see if I am real.
Those elongated lances of air escape through spaces
in the shaft's joints and chill me like xylophone notes.
I wasn't even leaving the airport
to enter fields of snow. I was merely connecting.
So I move the gray woollen coat from my arm
and put it on. I enter the lobby that's light with traffic.
I'm England bound. I'm bound, by history,
to every dimension of cold.

Airborne, I continue with Morrison's *Jazz*:
Malvonne wrenched with sorrow for the Bajan Winsome Clark
whose husband in Panama sends money that's intercepted
and never reaches her. She and the children drown with insufficiency.
Her hope rests in images of Bajan sunshine and big trees.
I'm not Winsome Clark, but I too know the chilly fingers
of deprivation, of calculated disinterest, of dripping indifference,
of whirling around with no systems of support,
of the loneliness penetrating drop by drop
that makes us playboys, patrons of nude dance halls, midnight cruisers.
Just to be near humans,
just to hear human voices,
just to feel some momentary warmth
we know will flee by sunrise.

The true value of planes is that, suspended between
heaven and earth, in neutral space, strangers may unite
for a few hours, may speak their despair,
knowing they won't see each other again, knowing
judgement won't follow them. They speak
candidly of divorces, racism, flying phobias,

or lighter subjects like good love and music.
"Where has all the good music gone to?" my
pharmaceuticalling neighbour says. "Oh, the eighties and nineties
produced one or two good individuals, but the seventies, man,
that was a renaissance. Every race, every nation, was producing great bands."
"Oh yes," I say. "All those great folk singers and R & B bands.
And don't forget Bob Marley."
Tension broken, I sleep solidly for an hour,
something I've never done while flying.
I felt there was something perversely indifferent
in sleeping at thirty thousand feet while
hurtling through air at hundreds of miles per hour.
Did I lack faith? Was indifference true faith,
knowing that, once suspended, having lost all personal control,
there was little point in worrying?

I would sleep even longer on the train from Heathrow to Leeds,
and I've slept like a child in a speeding car.
In train or car one's closer to the comforting earth.
Heaven's interstates are suited for the trafficking of souls.
Still I reflect on that sleeping hour up there,
that hour of returning faith.

PUJA CEREMONY

The gold-coated bell, hanging from a chain, sounds
another arrivant. Each link endlessly echoes karma,
the cycles of birth and death. A woman's quadrophonic voice chants
Lord Krishna's one thousand names. Those who are unable
repeat a single closing verse three times to receive
the same benefit as those who recited each name.
A tamboura's drone accompanies the woman's sitar voice,
hypnotic, devoted, disciplined, peaceful, a verbal liberation of the atman.

From their arched cubicles, seated Gods and Goddesses gaze
with identical smiling faces towards each mortal,
genders distinguished by colour of garment only:
males in white, females in purple: Shiva; Radha-Krishna;
elephantine Ganesha, remover of obstacles, over whom hangs
Om, the root of all words, recited in the sloka of the Gita;
Sita-Rama; six-armed Durga seated on a lion, the ego,
whose harmless roar curves from behind her;
Mahavira, 24th enlightened saint of Jainism.
A red gold-embroidered curtain is drawn across the first cubicle,
hiding its occupant. Men's arms and bodies flicker from behind that veil,
very active, business-like. Some hands carry towels; others sponge mops.
One, with a skillet, moves in full view across the line of idols
spilling a mixture of milk, water, honey, yogurt, and sugar around
each successive god. Others mop and polish, dhotis
tightly wrapped around their lower bodies.

The droning chant. The nostril-invading incense.
The hanging arrivants' bell no longer ringing.
Three women in saris glide towards the idols with bowls of fruit
topped with coconut. Fervently, they place
each bowl by the feet of the gods, make Catholic-like signs
across their chests, take their seats on the carpeted temple floor.
Three men approach laden with canteens of freshly-cooked food
placed next to the fruit. Now a collusion of thickly-scented incense
and cooked food takes the uninitiated

to a nauseous threshold. A sequence of plaques brimming with *Gita* quotes
surrounds the hall like a turban. *Surrender to Krishna's deliverance.*

A plate seems to float at will across the hall.
Communion fingers pucker up pieces of god food.
A mother prods her little boy stretched on the carpet.
She hoists his unwillingness, but he won't stand up,
keeps a dead weight of resistance that's finally conquered
by her stern looks and hefting hands.
She knows the hidden God is ready to be revealed.

Those who prepared him gather before the curtain
almost nervous with anticipation. Simultaneously,
as the curtain's drawn, peals of worship and praise and bells
rush toward Sri Venkateswara, a Krishna incarnation.
In even meter, a man throws food to the god.
Another paints him with fire leaping from a censer.
The epicentre of worship spills over like lava
before gradually receding into more sampling of god food,
informal chatting. The bell sounds again and again
announcing the end of each individual's devotion.
In the ante-chamber, bare feet find their shoes.

GLORY
(Augusta, Georgia. February 5, 1997)

On a cool bright afternoon,
amidst the chatter and laughter
of strangers and colleagues, we filed past
the cherry trees' petal-pink radiance into the complex.

The speaker, one eye hooked to the new century,
desired college education for all. For over an hour,
he developed ten points that sparkled with Hope
and tingled with applause.

Seeing him there was seeing him on screen:
the same calm affability, the didactic emollient,
the gray hair. The earnest face flushed with youth,
was an acorn shouldering southern soil.

When he finished, a throng lingered.
He shook every reaching hand,
spoke to others with sacramental grace.
A child stretched through the air

was a hyphen between two centuries.
The child proffered a card.
He took it, then waved to the crowd.
That gesture, reciprocated, fanned the air with the force of history.

He held that much power. I felt my own heart
crest with a bigness that brought the world in.
I thought of Gandhi, MLK, Mandela.
How their own gestures could make a nation.

I thought of Jesus, as popular, as thronged,
but who, unlike politician or priest,
gave healing to every outstretched hand
and peace to troubled rivers.

What if it were him standing behind that podium instead,
raising the dead with his word,
curing every imaginable disease?
How would this place contain such power?

DAY OF CONGREGATION
In the Name of Allah, the Compassionate, the Merciful

It squats unassumingly on Davant Street
away from the roar of fast foods, car dealerships,
and other wide-angled symbols of commerce,
a building modest as the covered heads and arms which entered
through the side door, seated now with patient expectation in their section.
The men close businesses or take lunch breaks for this weekly embrace,
a tryst that would only be broken through some unforeseen delay.
They quickly exit vehicles, briskly stride across the parking lot
to the mosque's main entrance. In the lobby, shoes removed
and placed in hive-like lockers mottling one wall, they glide,
with the smooth precision of habit, towards their own section.

The first call's for individual prayer.
Several men instantly drop to their knees, bottoms up,
foreheads touching the carpet, hands outstretched,
palms pressed to the floor. Others rock back and forth.
Each one has his own particular style of submission: prostrate sprawling,
standing with raised hands, sitting, squatting, kneeling.

A single door space visually links this section to the one behind
dotted with chairs that hold the women
each wrapped in graceful dupatta and salwar kameez.
On a prayer rug facing a wall, they too make supplications,
heads shawled in simplicity. Through the door space they glimpse
the men, but hear the priest's voice through speakers wired to their room.

One must think of Muhammad, long ago,
exiled, cunning, advancing for Mecca with justice and peace in mind.
One must think of all those Arabian tribes, after his death,
uniting and sweeping over Persian and Byzantine empires,
to alter the history of the world. Like Christianity, a life-style
accepted through the zeal of simple followers
or through the State's drawn sword.

Here, today, beauty reigns over political terror.
There're no physical pews, no racial barriers,
as Malcolm remarked after making his own journey.
But why the sections? Why the divide
between men and women?
Why the women stationed behind?
Men stand or sit in rows demarcated by white horizontal lines
that stretch across the hall like running tracks.
New arrivants prostrate as softly as curving waves.
The priest calls for surrender to Allah.

Along those latitudinal lines, there's no isolating inward craning.
Each person can touch the other, feel the other's breath.
The priest exorts, and they respond.
The music of their voices arc and circle like doves
then return to each heart for silent prayer.

TWO RULERS

It comes like a drawn blade into every heartland, into every interstate
of the imagination. Manipulation on the job and in love,
jockeying for power. Callouses sprout from its fingers
into the norm of our time. Yet, in spite of the winning, the having-it-our-way,
there's something large and empty that wouldn't let go.
A ruler rubs grinning palms. Under the shadow of his foot,
we joylessly squirm, separate yet pinned to each other with fear.
Another ruler sits, knowing. Had once conversed with the grinning king.
Momentarily wore the forked darkness like a cloak by which to save....
And so, thoughts pinned to pink petunias, multifarious
zinnias, and sparkling coreopsis; thoughts pinned
to the red plume of a cardinal bathing in a pool of light,
thoughts pinned to the yellow-breast perched on a brown wooden fence,
will invalidate the tarnishers of love, not love itself.
Sure, someone went weeping with sunstroke,
someone, encircled with pollen, roared with allergenic rage.
But who can deny the faithfulness of the sun,
it's pollinating glitter that gives life, that engenders peace?

SONG OF FAITH

By faith in God, my mountains fall.
By faith in God, I fall and rise again.
Tidal waves dwindle and die;
macajuels dare not touch my body.
And I sing and sing and sing,
hallelujah, hallelujah, hallelujah.

By faith, I gouge the eyes of a gorgon.
By faith, demonic mouths are sealed.
A poised centipede, green with venom,
glistens, then back-peddles into the dark.
And I sing and sing and sing,
hallelujah, hallelujah, hallelujah.

I override the stare of the nearness of Satan.
I over-climb the fear of the height of the mountain.
And I sing and sing and sing,
hallelujah, hallelujah, hallelujah.
And I sing and sing and sing,
hallelujah, hallelujah, hallelujah.

atman: the Hindu's individual self

dupatta: head covering worn by Muslim women.

karma: the Hindu belief that actions involve consequences that must be suffered through many lives.

Janus and *Tawarawa:* Roman and African gods, respectively, with the ability to look in opposite directions at once.

khus-khus: long bladed grass often used to border property.

macajuels: snakes found in the Caribbean.

Morrison: African-American author, Toni Morrison.

Nanny Grigg: On April 14th, 1816, in the south eastern parish of St. Philip, Nanny Grigg and other slaves, led by Bussa, orchestrated Barbados' largest slave revolt. Nanny Grigg played an enormous role. As a house slave who could read, she kept the other slaves abreast of developments of the Haitian revolution, an event that had inspired them and other slaves throughout the Caribbean.

Osibisa, Donovan, Labi Siffre, Cat Stevens: British pop musicians of the 1970s. Siffre and the members of Osibisa have African origins.

puja: prayer and worship.

salwar kameez: Muslim pants and shirt.

sloka: one of two meters used in the *Bhagavad-Gita.*

tamboura: Hindu four or five-stringed instrument.

Tuk: the indigenous folk music of Barbados created during the colonial period by slaves who fused the rhythms of the British marching bands with the rhythms of their African ancestors. Also called Ruk-a-tuk. Wayne "Poonka" Willock is the contemporary champion of Tuk music and is the first person to incorporate it into Barbadian calypso. A Tuk group normally comprises a bass drum, a snare drum, a flute or penny whistle, and a triangle.

Several of the poems in this book are written in the three formats of the author's invention, Tuk Verse. The meters of Tuk Verse are drawn from the vocal melody of the early Tuk song, from the vocal melody of the Tuk calypso, and from snare drum patterns. These Tuk Verse poems, respectively, are 'Chenille'; 'Islander'; and 'Pressure', 'Death of an Uncle', and 'Rainbow of Sand'. 'Coming Home' uses all three Tuk Verse formats in addition to exploratory form.

ABOUT THE AUTHOR

Anthony Kellman was born in Barbados and educated there and in the U.S.A. At eighteen he left for Britain where he worked as a troubadour playing pop and West Indian folk music on the pub and folk club circuit. He now lives in the U.S.A. where he is a professor of English and creative writing at Augusta State University, Georgia. In 1992 he edited the first full-length U.S. anthology of English-Speaking Caribbean poetry, *Crossing Water*. A recipient of a National Endowment for the Arts fellowship, his poetry, fiction and critical essays have appeared in journals all over the world.

ALSO BY TONY KELLMAN

The Coral Rooms 0 948833 53 X £5.95

Percival Veer has risen to the 10th floor of the Federal Bank of Charouga, has acquired a large and imposing house and a young and attentive wife. But satisfaction eludes him. Guilt over a past wrong begins to trouble him and a recurring dream of caves disturbs his sleep. As Percy's world crumbles, he is gripped by an obsessive desire to explore the deep limestone caves of his island, dimly remembered from his boyhood.

Watercourse 0 948833 37 8 £5.99

Edouard Glissant wrote: "Anthony Kellman's poetry has the strength and sweetness of vegetation with the power of progressively revealing to us the nature of the earth in which it grows."

The Long Gap 0 948833 78 5 £5.95

Nancy Willard wrote: "Anthony Kellman's poetry combines the rhythms of Caribbean music with a splendid gift for metaphor and form. You will find yourself wanting to read these poems out loud."